D0482571

Sometimes, You Just Have To Make Your OWN Rules

A LUANN BOOK BY GREG EVANS

Rutledge Hill Press
Nashville, Tennessee

Published in Nashville, Tennessee, by Rutledge Hill Press, Inc., 211 Seventh Avenue North, Nashville, Tennessee 37219. Distributed in Canada by H. B. Fenn & Company, Ltd., 34 Nixon Road, Bolton, Ontario L7E 1W2. Distributed in Australia by The Five Mile Press Pty., Ltd., 22 Summit Road, Noble Park, Victoria 3174. Distributed in New Zealand by Tandem Press, 2 Rugby Road, Birkenhead, Auckland 10. Distributed in the United Kingdom by Verulam Publishing, Ltd., 152a Park Street Lane, Park Street, St. Albans, Hertfordshire AL2 2AU.

Library of Congress Cataloging in Publication Data is available.
ISBN 1-55853-616-7

Printed in China

1 2 3 4 5 6 7 8 9   03 02 01 00 99 98

Sometimes, You Just Have To Make Your OWN Rules

Sometimes, you just have to make your OWN rules.

Most "rules"
are WAY too
practical.

Morning starts too early.
Let's move it to noon.

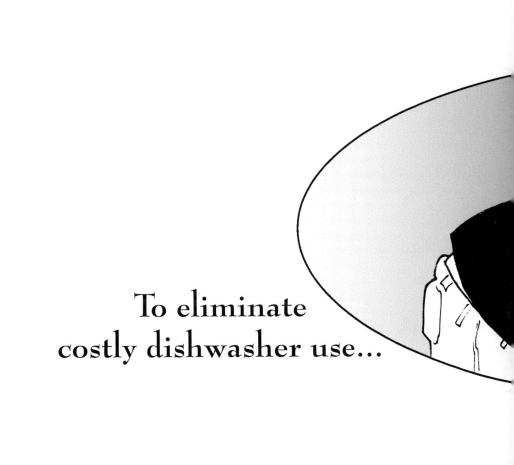

To eliminate
costly dishwasher use...

...eat directly from the fridge.

Every now and then,
rattle someone's cage.

Do unto others because they'll sure do unto you.

Remember:
Your stuff is YOUR stuff.
Your parent's stuff
is your stuff, too.

Mumbling is often the best strategy.

If you can't have a brainstorm, try for scattered showers.

Luann's Food Fact:

There's as much vitamin C in 13 servings of vanilla ice cream as in one serving of asparagus.

When you
know what
you want,
SAY so!

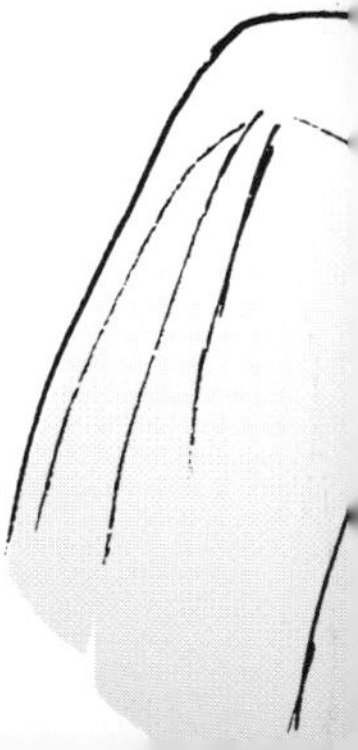

You don't have
to be tidy to be
organized.

Couch potatoes
don't have stress.

There IS no rule about correct furniture usage.

"NO" is an
excellent
word.
Use it
often.

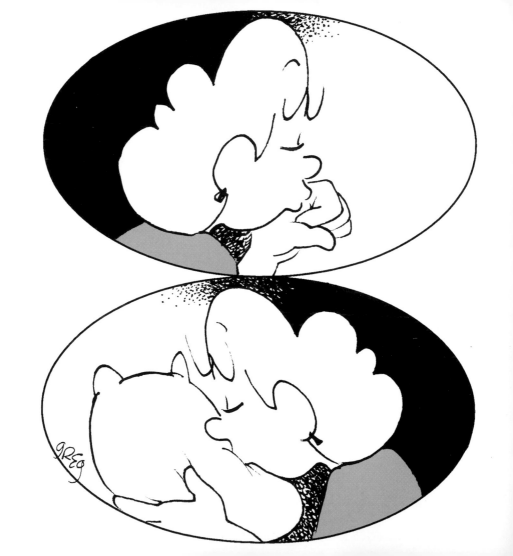

You can try...

...but there's just no good way
to practice kissing.

Making your bed is not only pointless, it can seriously upset your life.

The more you know, the more you know how little you know.

Never argue
with your
tastebuds.

You'll always know
exactly what to do
after you've done it.

Despite what
experts say,
TV <u>does</u>
stimulate
conversation.

Early to bed, early to rise.
Ha Ha Ha.

Scientists need to seriously work on finding a cure for pillow face.

True romance
is hard to find.

Just make
your own.

The secret to success is knowing how to turn a liability into an asset.

Just accept it:
your body has
too much hair
and your hair
has no body.

There's always an easier way
to do any job.

Just because you need everything you have doesn't mean you have everything you need.

PLEASE PLEASE PLEASE
PLEASE PLEEEEEASE
PLEASEPLEASEPLEASE
PUH-LEEEZE
PLEASE PLEASE
GREG

You can't
always get
what you want.
But, hey,
don't let THAT
stop you.

Drive-thru gyms
are a must.

Eat three well-rounded meals daily:
donuts for breakfast,
cookies for lunch,
pizza for dinner.

No matter how big your wardrobe is, it's too small.

Getting away
from it all
is great.

Just take
some of it
with you.

One person's dream
is another person's
nightmare.

A penny saved is a
penny earned.
Big woop.
Like THAT
helps.

There is <u>nothing</u> wrong
with giving up and
going back to bed.

Midnight snacking
is perfectly fine.
Why else is there
a light in the fridge?

If you look around,
you can always find
a job to do.
Obviously,
you shouldn't
look around.

Planning ahead is a waste of time. I mean, did <u>your</u> day go how you planned it?

Besides 14 vacation days,
10 sick days and
2 mental health days...

..let's have 24 bad-hair days.

If you set your goals low enough,
you'll always be successful.

What you WANT to eat and what there IS to eat never match up.

Your stuff is stuff.
Everyone else's stuff
is junk.

Silence is golden.
Gossip is Fort Knox.

The big weekend you imagine on Wednesday rarely shows up on Saturday.

Most of what you read
on food labels has no
connection to real life.

With a little practice,
you can learn to blame everything
on the opposite sex.

Today's "must-haves" are tomorrow's "must-goes."

There are 130,000 items in the supermarket, yet there's never anything to eat.

"Thinking outside the box"
is encouraged but
not appreciated.

One trip to the store
is never enough.

If you know
what color your
bedroom carpet is,
you're WAY
too neat.

The early bird
catches the worm.

This is an
excellent
reason to
sleep late.

No matter how old you get,
you'll never know what
you're doing.

Just fake it like
everyone else.

Now and then,
your horoscope
will be right on...
and WAY off.

Virgo

This weekend,
you'll experience
some hot n' heavy
action!

Eat 5 servings of fruit and vegetables daily.

Today's Menu:
Corn dog, potato chips, onion rings, cherry coke, strawberry ice cream.

WHOOF

Everything's
better after
a good hug.

Whatever you're
doing, make it
look harder
than it is.

If you really apply yourself, you can find a way around any rule.